Reviewing Early American History Handbook with Activities

HOLT, RINEHART AND WINSTON

A Harcourt Education Company

Austin · New York · Orlando · Atlanta · San Francisco · Boston · Dallas · Toronto · London

ISBN 0-03-065341-X

8 9 10 11 12 082 09 08 07 06 05

Contents

Reviewing Early American History Activities

TO THE TEACHER

Reviewing Early American History Activities provides multipart activities to help students review American history before 1877. These activities will help students prepare for assessment exams as well allow you to teach quickly a great deal of material. Each activity covers a distinct time period in American history, starting with the earliest Americans and ending with Reconstruction.

Name _____ Class _____ Date _____

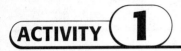
The World by 1500

Key Points

- The first Americans came from Asia between 12,000 and 40,000 years ago and over time created distinct cultures throughout the Americas.

- Trade contributed to the spread of cultures and ideas in Asia and Africa prior to the 1500s, but European involvement in trade over the centuries was somewhat uneven.

- During the Middle Ages, feudal kingdoms, independent city-states, and church-controlled lands gradually gave way to nation-states in most of western Europe.

- New technology and the desire to find an all-sea route to the East spurred exploration in the 1400s, with Portugal leading the way.

Reviewing Main Ideas

MULTIPLE CHOICE For each of the following, place the letter of the best choice in the space provided.

_____ **1.** These people followed animal herds across Beringia to North America.
  a. Mound Builders
  b. Olmec
  c. Paleo-Indians
  d. Toltec

_____ **2.** They improved algebra, refined the concept of zero, and advanced mapmaking.
  a. Muslims
  b. Africans
  c. Vikings
  d. Chinese

_____ **3.** During the Crusades, Christians fought against Muslims for control of this area.
  a. the Indies
  b. the Iberian Peninsula
  c. Ghana
  d. Palestine

_____ **4.** This person earned the title *la Católica* for promoting Catholicism in Spain.
  a. Queen Isabella
  b. Prince Henry
  c. Bartolomeu Dias
  d. King Ferdinand

_____ **5.** Millions of Africans were enslaved and forced from their native lands, which led to the African
  a. Renaissance.
  b. *Reconquista.*
  c. Diaspora.
  d. Revolution.

_____ **6.** He established an all-water East-West trade route.
  a. Kublai Khan
  b. Vasco da Gama
  c. Leif Eriksson
  d. Mansa Musa

Name ______________________ Class ______________ Date ______________

Activity 1, Reviewing Early American History, continued

SHORT ANSWER Provide brief answers for each of the following. Remember to use examples to support your answer.

1. What changes were brought about by the Agricultural Revolution?

____

____

2. How did trade affect the growth of Asia and Africa?

____

____

3. How did the marriage of Isabella and Ferdinand help reshape Spain?

____

____

4. Why was an eastern sea route to Asia so important to the Europeans?

____

____

ORGANIZING INFORMATION

Complete the following chart by listing the locations and accomplishments of the culture groups shown.

Cultures	Locations	Accomplishments
Olmec		
Maya		
Toltec		
Aztec		
Inca		
Anasazi		
Adena/Hopewell		

WRITING

Compose a short essay that answers the following question: How did technological advances help the Portuguese establish trade routes? In your answer, be sure to support your points with historical facts.

Name _____ Class _____ Date _____

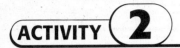

Reviewing Early American History

Empires of the Americas

Key Points

- Looking for direct western trade routes to Asia, Europeans found what later became known as North and South America.
- In the 1500s Spanish conquistadores conquered the Aztec and Inca Empires and began settlements in the Americas.
- Spain's influence in the Americas gradually declined, and other European countries began settling in North America.
- England experienced first failure and then success in its attempt to build a permanent settlement in North America.

Reviewing Main Ideas

TRUE/FALSE Mark each statement *T* if it is true or *F* if it is false.

_____ **1.** In 1492 Christopher Columbus landed on a tiny island in the Bahama Islands and named it San Salvador.

_____ **2.** Under the *encomienda* system, Spanish colonists worked for their American Indian neighbors in exchange for food and gold.

_____ **3.** The Spanish began importing African slaves in the early 1500s.

_____ **4.** Ferdinand Magellan's expedition was the first to circumnavigate the world.

_____ **5.** San Diego is the oldest city established by Europeans in the present-day United States.

_____ **6.** Spanish demands that the Pueblo pay taxes and convert to Catholicism led to the Pueblo Revolt.

_____ **7.** Spain organized its territory into large provinces called peons.

_____ **8.** The Protestant Revolution began when Martin Luther protested against corruption in the Protestant church.

_____ **9.** No one knows for sure why the English settlers of Roanoke disappeared.

_____ **10.** Jamestown, the first permanent English settlement in North America, was founded in 1607.

Name _____ Class _____ Date _____

SHORT ANSWER Provide brief answers for each of the following. Remember to use examples to support your answer.

1. How did Bartolomé de Las Casas view the *encomienda* system?

   _____

   _____

2. What attracted Spanish explorers to the Americas?

   _____

   _____

3. What role did the Catholic Church play in Spanish exploration and settlement of the Americas?

   _____

   _____

4. How did tobacco affect the history of Jamestown?

   _____

   _____

ORGANIZING INFORMATION

For each explorer listed below, identify the people encountered by that explorer and the result of the encounter.

Explorer	People Encountered	Result
Christopher Columbus		
Ferdinand Magellan		
Hernán Cortés		
Francisco Pizarro		

WRITING

Compose a short essay that answers the following question: Why did Christopher Columbus believe he could reach Asia by sailing west? In your answer, be sure to support your points with historical facts.

Name _____ Class _____ Date _____

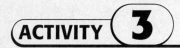 **Reviewing Early American History**

The English Colonies

Key Points

- In the early 1600s many Puritans left England for North America in search of religious freedom.
- Conflicts in the Massachusetts Bay Colony led some colonists to leave and establish new colonies elsewhere.
- The reliance of the southern economy on agriculture gradually led to the institutionalization of slavery.
- The Glorious Revolution and the Great Awakening led to the founding of new colonies and new religious faiths.

Reviewing Main Ideas

MATCHING In the space provided, write the historical term identified by each description. Choose your answers from the list below. There is one extra term on the list.

Fundamental Orders of Connecticut	Great Awakening	Great Migration
House of Burgesses	Enlightenment	Toleration Act
Glorious Revolution	Mayflower Compact	Middle Passage

_____ **1.** established a self-governing colony

_____ **2.** period during which more than 40,000 Puritans left England for the Americas to escape religious persecution

_____ **3.** first written constitution in the colonies

_____ **4.** passed to protect Maryland's Catholic minority

_____ **5.** Virginia's assembly, which limited the governor's power

_____ **6.** voyage of enslaved Africans across the Atlantic Ocean

_____ **7.** revolution in ideas that emphasized human reason as the key to improving society

_____ **8.** series of religious revivals that swept through the British colonies in the mid-1700s

SHORT ANSWER Provide brief answers for each of the following. Remember to use examples to support your answer.

1. What was the New England Way?

_____

_____

Activity 3, Reviewing Early American History, continued

2. Why did some people leave the Massachusetts Bay Colony?

_____

_____

3. How did early colonists react to the institution of slavery?

_____

_____

4. How did England's Glorious Revolution affect the colonies?

_____

_____

ORGANIZING INFORMATION

For each colony listed below, identify the person or group that settled the colony and the reason the colony was established.

Colony	Settled by	Reason for Colony
Plymouth		
Massachusetts Bay		
Connecticut		
Providence		
Maryland		
The Carolinas		
New York/New Jersey		
Pennsylvania		
Georgia		

WRITING

Compose a short essay that answers the following question: How did economics shape the early history of the Chesapeake? In your answer, be sure to support your points with historical facts.

Name _____ Class _____ Date _____

The Struggle for Land

Key Points

- Although France claimed a huge area of North America, New France never reached its potential strength.
- The European desire for furs and land led to conflicts between European settlers and American Indians.
- Worldwide struggles for empire by European countries often spilled over into North America, dragging English colonists into three wars between 1689 and 1748.
- The French and Indian War first broke out in the Ohio River valley, an area highly valued by both the French and the British.
- The Treaty of Paris of 1763 formally ended the war, with victory for the British.

Reviewing Main Ideas

FILL IN THE BLANK In the space provided, write the name of the person or the historical term that will complete each sentence. Choose your answers from the list below. There is one extra name or term on the list.

Albany Plan of Union	French and Indian War	Metacomet
Montreal	New Orleans	Jacques Cartier
James Wolfe	William Pitt	Iroquois League

1. The early voyages of Giovanni da Verrazano and _____ provided the basis for French land claims in North America.

2. The founding of _____ in 1718 gave the French control of the Mississippi River.

3. In 1675 Wampanoag chief _____ led American Indians in war against the English settlers.

4. The _____ was a confederation formed by the Cayuga, Mohawk, Oneida, Onondaga, and Seneca, and later joined by the Tuscarora.

5. Benjamin Franklin proposed the _____ to unite the colonies in a loose confederation for defense.

6. The _____ began in the colonies in 1754 and spread to Europe in 1756.

7. The British built a new fort near the site of Fort Duquesne and named it after British cabinet minister _____ .

8. When _____ fell to the British in 1760, France lost the last of its Canadian holdings.

Activity 4, Reviewing Early American History, continued

SHORT ANSWER Provide brief answers for each of the following. Remember to use examples to support your answer.

1. Why did France settle so little of the land it claimed in North America?

_____

_____

2. How did the Iroquois League benefit its members?

_____

_____

3. What led to a British victory in the French and Indian War?

_____

_____

4. What did Britain gain from its victory in the French and Indian War?

_____

_____

ORGANIZING INFORMATION

Complete the chart below by comparing the European view of land with the American Indian view of land.

How Europeans Viewed Land	How American Indians Viewed Land

WRITING

Compose a short essay that answers the following question: How did the European desire for furs change life for many American Indians? In your answer, be sure to support your points with historical facts.

Name _____ Class _____ Date _____

ACTIVITY **5**   Reviewing Early American History
                                    Independence!

Key Points

- On April 19, 1775, after years of tension between colonists and the British government, fighting broke out in Massachusetts at the Battle of Lexington.

- On July 4, 1776, members of the Continental Congress approved the Declaration of Independence creating the United States of America.

- In October 1777 the Patriots won a major victory at Saratoga, which marked a turning point in the war.

- In October 1781 the British surrender at the Battle of Yorktown secured the American victory in the war.

- The Treaty of Paris of 1783 formally ended the war.

Reviewing Main Ideas

MULTIPLE CHOICE For each of the following, place the letter of the best choice in the space provided.

_____ **1.** This radical group protested British rule.
   a. Loyalists
   b. Olive Branchers
   c. Sons of Liberty
   d. The Opposition

_____ **2.** Which battle is associated with Washington's crossing of the Delaware?
   a. Saratoga
   b. Yorktown
   c. Trenton
   d. Bunker Hill

_____ **3.** His pamphlet *Common Sense* stirred up support for the Revolution.
   a. Thomas Paine
   b. Patrick Henry
   c. George Washington
   d. John Adams

_____ **4.** This 33-year-old did most of the actual writing of the Declaration of Independence.
   a. Thomas Paine
   b. Thomas Jefferson
   c. Richard Henry Lee
   d. John Adams

_____ **5.** This 19-year-old French nobleman became an important member of Washington's staff.
   a. Marquis de Lafayette
   b. Francis Marion
   c. John Burgoyne
   d. François de Grasse

_____ **6.** American victory in this battle convinced France to join the fight against Britain.
   a. Lexington
   b. Saratoga
   c. Bunker Hill
   d. Yorktown

Name _____ Class _____ Date _____

SHORT ANSWER Provide brief answers for each of the following. Remember to use examples to support your answer.

1. How did the Intolerable Acts anger the colonists?

_____

_____

2. Why did the colonists become opposed to British rule?

_____

_____

3. What advantages did the small Continental Army have over the well-trained British army?

_____

_____

4. How did colonists respond when independence was declared?

_____

_____

ORGANIZING INFORMATION

Use the following cause-and-effect graphic organizer to list at least three causes and three outcomes of the American Revolution.

Causes of the Revolution	**Outcomes of the Revolution**

WRITING

Compose a short essay that answers the following question: How did the participation of European allies affect the Revolutionary War? In your answer, be sure to support your points with historical facts.

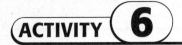 **Reviewing Early American History**

91 Worksheet Title

Key Points

- Between 1776 and 1780 the states adopted state constitutions that addressed the major colonial concerns.
- On November 15, 1777, Congress adopted the Articles of Confederation, which joined the states in an association but allowed them to keep most of the power.
- Government under the Articles of Confederation resolved many of the nation's land issues but had few other successes.
- The weaknesses of government under the Articles of Confederation convinced many people that a stronger central government was needed.

Reviewing Main Ideas

TRUE/FALSE Mark each statement *T* if it is true or *F* if it is false.

_____ **1.** Under republicanism, political leaders receive from the citizens their authority to make and enforce laws.

_____ **2.** The state legislatures were influenced by Enlightenment philosopher John Locke's belief that all people are born with natural rights.

_____ **3.** The Mayflower Compact provided American leaders with a model of self-government.

_____ **4.** The Articles of Confederation created an American monarchy.

_____ **5.** The easiest way for Congress to raise money under the Articles of Confederation was to tax tobacco consumption.

_____ **6.** The Articles created a weak central government because early American leaders wanted to prevent abuse of power by a central authority.

_____ **7.** The Northwest Ordinance established a process by which territories could become states.

_____ **8.** Proposed changes to the Articles required the consent of 9 of the 13 states.

_____ **9.** One cause of the depression of 1784 was the loss of British markets.

_____ **10.** Shays's Rebellion led many people to call for a less powerful central government.

Activity 6, Reviewing Early American History, continued

SHORT ANSWER Provide brief answers for each of the following. Remember to use examples to support your answer.

1. How did colonial experiences influence the way the state constitutions were written?

_____

_____

2. How did the Virginia Statute for Religious Freedom protect individual rights?

_____

_____

3. What land issues did the new Congress resolve?

_____

_____

4. How did the government's economic policies lead to Shays's Rebellion?

_____

_____

ORGANIZING INFORMATION

Complete the chart below by listing four powers of Congress under the Articles of Confederation and four weaknesses of government under the Articles of Confederation.

Powers of Congress	Weaknesses of Government
_____	_____
_____	_____
_____	_____
_____	_____

WRITING

Compose a short essay that answers the following question: How effective were the Articles of Confederation in carrying out the ideals of the Declaration of Independence—particularly that of "Life, Liberty, and the Pursuit of Happiness? In your answer, be sure to support your points with historical facts.

Name _____ Class _____ Date _____

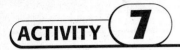 **ACTIVITY 7**   Reviewing Early American History

The U.S. Constitution

Key Points

- In May 1787, delegates at the Constitutional Convention began working on ways to strengthen the U.S. government.
- The final version of the U.S. Constitution, containing a number of important compromises, was signed in September 1787 and sent to Congress and then to the states for ratification.
- Federalists and Antifederalists battled over the issues of individual rights and a strong central government versus states' rights, but in 1790 ratification was narrowly approved.
- The U.S. Constitution is a living, flexible document that has endured for more than 200 years.

Reviewing Main Ideas

MATCHING In the space provided, write the historical term identified by each description. Choose your answers from the list below. There is one extra term on the list.

   separation of powers   checks and balances   federalism
   concurrent powers   reserved powers   supremacy clause
   elastic clause   delegated powers   veto

_____ **1.** division of powers between a strong central government and the state governments

_____ **2.** powers given to the federal government by the Constitution, such as the power to regulate trade

_____ **3.** powers guaranteed to the states by the Tenth Amendment to the Constitution

_____ **4.** powers held jointly by the federal government and the state governments, such as the power to levy taxes

_____ **5.** clause in the Constitution that ranks the Constitution and federal laws above state constitutions and state laws

_____ **6.** refers to the fact that each branch of government enjoys specific powers the other branches cannot claim

_____ **7.** system that gives each branch of government the means to restrain the powers of the other two branches

_____ **8.** allows Congress to exert its powers in ways not specifically outlined in the Constitution

Activity 7, Reviewing Early American History, continued

SHORT ANSWER Provide brief answers for each of the following. Remember to use examples to support your answer.

1. What were the differences between the Virginia Plan and the New Jersey Plan?

_____

_____

2. What was *The Federalist,* and what was its purpose?

_____

_____

3. Why did the framers of the Constitution establish a system of checks and balances?

_____

_____

4. Why can it be said that the Constitution is a "living document"?

_____

_____

ORGANIZING INFORMATION

Use the following graphic organizer to identify the main arguments used by Antifederalists and Federalists concerning ratification of the Constitution.

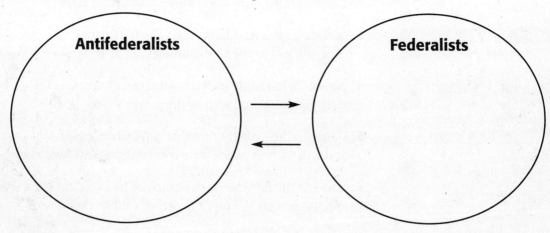

WRITING

Compose a short essay that answers the following question: What major compromises were reached at the Constitutional Convention? In your answer, be sure to support your points with historical facts.

Name _____ Class _____ Date _____

Key Points

- In 1789, newly elected government officials—the president and members of Congress—set out to put the Constitution into action.

- Alexander Hamilton strengthened the nation's economy as settlement in the Northwest Territory led to conflict with American Indians.

- The French Revolution of 1789 threatened to pull the United States into an international conflict.

- In the mid-1790s international conflicts and sectionalism contributed to the rise of political parties in the United States, which played an important role in the election of 1796.

Reviewing Main Ideas

FILL IN THE BLANK In the space provided, write the name of the person or the historical term that will complete each sentence. Choose your answers from the list below. There is one extra name or term on the list.

Little Turtle	Alexander Hamilton	John Adams
strict construction	loose construction	Judiciary
Democratic-Republican	George Washington	Federalist

1. _____ was unanimously chosen to be the first president.

2. The _____ Act of 1789 established a federal district court for each state.

3. Secretary of the Treasury _____ advised Congress to strengthen the nation's credit by beginning to pay off the national debt.

4. Thomas Jefferson felt that the government could do only what the Constitution

specifically allows, a philosophy known as _____.

5. In 1791, warriors led by Miami chief _____ defeated U.S. troops in a battle along the Wabash River in present-day Indiana.

6. The _____ Party, led by Alexander Hamilton, found support among merchants, manufacturers, lawyers, and church leaders from New England and the Atlantic seaboard.

7. Planters, small farmers, wage earners, artisans, and tradespeople tended to support the _____ Party, led by Thomas Jefferson.

8. In 1796 _____ became the second U.S. president.

Activity 8, Reviewing Early American History, continued

SHORT ANSWER Provide brief answers for each of the following. Remember to use examples to support your answer.

1. Contrast the views of Hamilton and Jefferson concerning the Bank of the United States.

_____

2. How did Americans react to the French Revolution?

_____

3. How were the Alien and Sedition Acts contrary to the Bill of Rights?

_____

ORGANIZING INFORMATION

Complete the chart below by identifying which amendment in the Bill of Rights is being described in the left column.

Rights and Freedoms	Amendment
right to a speedy trial, to counsel, to question witnesses, to know charges	1. _____ Amendment
reserves for states and people powers not given to the national government or prohibited by the Constitution	2. _____ Amendment
right to bear arms	3. _____ Amendment
right to a jury trial in most civil cases	4. _____ Amendment
protects rights not specifically mentioned in Constitution	5. _____ Amendment
prohibits cruel and unusual punishment, excessive fines and bail	6. _____ Amendment
freedom of speech, religion, press, assembly, and petition	7. _____ Amendment
prohibits unlawful searches and seizures	8. _____ Amendment
guarantees due process of law	9. _____ Amendment
prohibits forced quartering of troops	10. _____ Amendment

WRITING

Compose a short essay that answers the following question: What tasks did the new Congress complete during its first session? In your answer, be sure to support your points with historical facts.

Name _____ Class _____ Date _____

 **Reviewing Early American History**

Expansion and War

Key Points

- In 1803 the United States completed the Louisiana Purchase, the largest land deal in history.
- Explorations in the early 1800s provided Americans with information about U.S. territory west of the Mississippi River.
- International and domestic conflicts led the United States into war with Britain in 1812.
- Although the Treat of Ghent ended the war, neither side gained much.

Reviewing Main Ideas

TRUE/FALSE Mark each statement *T* if it is true or *F* if it is false.

_____ **1.** The Twelfth Amendment, ratified in 1804, requires electors to vote for presidential and vice presidential candidates on separate ballots.

_____ **2.** Chief Justice John Marshall established the principle of judicial review—the power of the courts to declare an act of Congress unconstitutional.

_____ **3.** France sold the Louisiana Territory to the United States for $150 million.

_____ **4.** Lewis and Clark were unable to explore the Louisiana Territory because of continuing conflicts with the American Indians who lived there.

_____ **5.** The explorations of Zebulon Pike helped spur expansion into Texas and the Southwest.

_____ **6.** The Embargo Act of 1807 stopped shipments of food and other European products to American ports.

_____ **7.** The United States declared war on France on 1812.

_____ **8.** U.S. victory in the battle of the Thames broke the British hold on the Northwest Territory.

_____ **9.** The Battle of New Orleans was the most decisive U.S. victory in the war.

_____**10.** The Treaty of Ghent resulted in a peace between the United States and Britain that marked the beginning of a long partnership.

Activity 9, Reviewing Early American History, continued

SHORT ANSWER Provide brief answers for each of the following. Remember to use examples to support your answer.

1. How did the presidential election of 1800 differ from previous elections?

_____

2. Why did Napoléon Bonaparte want to sell the Louisiana Territory?

_____

3. How did the Embargo Act of 1807 weaken the U.S. economy?

_____

4. How did the congressional vote on whether to declare war on Great Britain reflect sectional tensions?

_____

ORGANIZING INFORMATION

Use the graphic organizer below to list the events that led to the outbreak of the War of 1812.

| **1.** Great Britain passes the Orders in Council. |
| **2.** |
| **3.** |
| **4.** |
| **5.** |
| **6.** |
| **7.** Congress declares war on Great Britain. |

WRITING

Compose a short essay that answers the following question: What was the significance of the Louisiana Purchase for the United States? In your answer, be sure to support your points with historical facts.

 Reviewing Early American History

Nationalism and Economic Growth

Key Points

- The War of 1812 inspired nationalism in the United States, and President James Monroe strove to bring harmony to foreign relations.
- The Market Revolution, Industrial Revolution, and Transportation Revolution changed the way Americans worked and lived.
- The election of Andrew Jackson to the presidency in 1828 enhanced the democratic nature of politics in the United States but had serious consequences for American Indians.
- States' rights, the Bank of the United States, and a faltering economy were controversial issues in the late 1820s and 1830s.

Reviewing Main Ideas

MATCHING In the space provided, write the historical term identified by each description. Choose your answers from the list below. There is one extra term on the list.

Industrial Revolution	Adams-Onís Treaty	Indian Removal Act
Missouri Compromise	Trail of Tears	First Seminole War
Market Revolution	*Worcester* v. *Georgia*	American System

_____ **1.** U.S.–American Indian conflict in Florida

_____ **2.** agreement in which Spain transferred East Florida to the United States

_____ **3.** Henry Clay's plan to create a national bank, a protective tariff, and a national transportation system

_____ **4.** increased farmers' and manufacturers' profits and changed the way they worked and did business

_____ **5.** period of dynamic changes in manufacturing

_____ **6.** agreement that admitted Missouri to the Union as a slave state and admitted Maine as a free state

_____ **7.** provided for the relocation of Indian tribes living east of the Mississippi River to Indian Territory

_____ **8.** forced relocation of the Cherokee people during which an estimated 4,000 Cherokee died

Name _____ Class _____ Date _____

SHORT ANSWER Provide brief answers for each of the following. Remember to use examples to support your answer.

1. What was the Monroe Doctrine, and why did President Monroe issue it?

_____

_____

2. How did the Industrial Revolution affect the U.S. economy?

_____

_____

3. How did Andrew Jackson change the tone of politics in the United States?

_____

_____

4. Why did South Carolina threaten to secede from the Union in 1832?

_____

_____

ORGANIZING INFORMATION

Use the following graphic organizer to supply information about the Transportation Revolution in each of the categories shown.

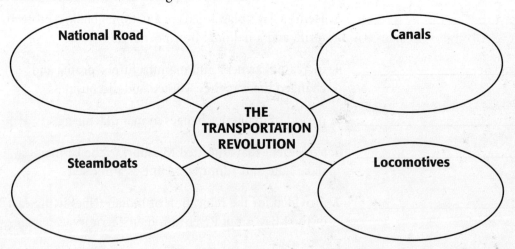

WRITING

Compose a short essay that answers the following question: What agreements did President James Monroe make with Great Britain? In your answer, be sure to support your points with historical facts.

Name _____ Class _____ Date _____

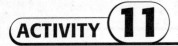
Regional Societies

Key Points

- Life in the United States changed dramatically between 1790 and 1860 as the North became more industrial and the South became more agricultural.
- In the North, the Industrial Revolution and the Market Revolution transformed industry and society.
- In the South, the invention of the cotton gin in the 1790s made cotton farming extremely profitable.
- The cotton boom led to the growing importance of slavery in the South.

Reviewing Main Ideas

FILL IN THE BLANK In the space provided, write the name of the person or the historical term that will complete each sentence. Choose your answers from the list below. There is one extra name or term on the list.

Tredegar Iron Works	yeoman farmers	Elias Howe
Eli Whitney	Cyrus McCormick	strike
African Americans	middle class	Market Revolution

1. During the early 1800s a(n) _____ arose, made up of prosperous artisans, farmers, lawyers, ministers, and shopkeepers.

2. _____ developed a mechanical reaper that could harvest six acres of grain in a day.

3. Labor unions sometimes went on _____, refusing to work until employers met union demands.

4. The _____ reduced the cost of manufactured products.

5. _____ invented the cotton gin in 1793.

6. The _____ of Richmond, Virginia, was one of the largest and best-equipped manufacturers of its kind in the nation.

7. _____ made up the majority of southern white society.

8. Free _____ in the South had to register with local authorities and carry identification passes proving they were not runaways.

Activity 11, Reviewing Early American History, continued

SHORT ANSWER Provide brief answers for each of the following. Remember to use examples to support your answer.

1. How did Francis Cabot Lowell contribute to manufacturing in the United States?

_____

_____

2. What kinds of restrictions did nativists try to impose on immigrants?

_____

_____

3. What was life like for poor whites in the South?

_____

_____

4. How did religion unite white southerners?

_____

_____

ORGANIZING INFORMATION

Complete the following Venn diagram, which outlines the reasons for Irish and German immigration to the United States.

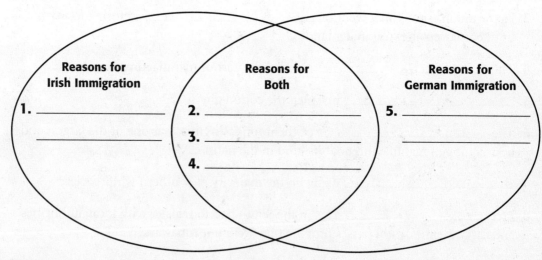

Reasons for Irish Immigration

1. _____

_____

Reasons for Both

2. _____

3. _____

4. _____

Reasons for German Immigration

5. _____

_____

WRITING

Compose a short essay that answers the following question: Why did industrialization develop more slowly in the South than in the North? In your answer, be sure to support your points with historical facts.

ACTIVITY 12   Reviewing Early American History

The Slave System

Key Points

- As cotton plantations spread throughout the South, the number of slaves in the South also grew.

- The lives of slaves varied depending on where they lived and what kind of owners they had, but all slaves had little say in what happened to themselves and their families.

- Slaves responded to their living and working conditions by developing a rich culture based on family bonds, art and music, and religion.

- Although they lacked legal power, African Americans found many ways to resist slavery.

Reviewing Main Ideas

MULTIPLE CHOICE For each of the following, place the letter of the best choice in the space provided.

_____ **1.** The number of slaves in the South had reached this figure by 1860.
   a. slightly more than 40,000
   b. approximately 400,000
   c. nearly 4 million
   d. around 40 million

_____ **2.** These slaves helped to supervise the work of other slaves.
   a. plowers
   b. conductors
   c. overseers
   d. drivers

_____ **3.** Slaves used linsey-woolsey to
   a. supplement their diet.
   b. treat their illnesses.
   c. pass messages to family members on other plantations.
   d. make their clothing.

_____ **4.** Slaves used this art form to chronicle their daily experiences.
   a. novels
   b. songs
   c. paintings
   d. plays

_____ **5.** This action was the most tempting form of resistance to slavery.
   a. faking illness
   b. damaging tools and other property
   c. running away
   d. setting fire to barns and other buildings

_____ **6.** This escaped slave led more than 300 slaves to freedom on the Underground Railroad.
   a. Harriet Tubman
   b. Denmark Vesey
   c. Gabriel Prosser
   d. Frederick Douglass

Activity 12, Reviewing Early American History, continued

SHORT ANSWER Provide brief answers for each of the following. Remember to use examples to support your answer.

1. What was the housing and diet of slaves like?

_____

_____

2. What role did oral history, folktales, and humor play in the lives of slaves?

_____

_____

3. How did religion help enslaved people endure slavery?

_____

_____

4. What was the Underground Railroad?

_____

_____

ORGANIZING INFORMATION

Use the following cause-and-effect graphic organizer to explain how Nat Turner's rebellion affected white southerners and slaves differently.

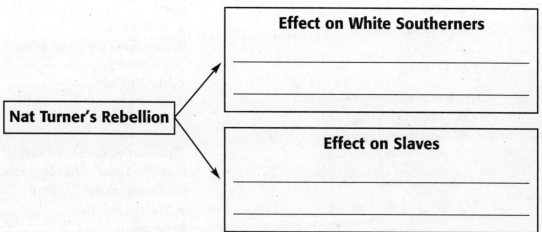

WRITING

Compose a short essay that answers the following question: How did slavery's critics and supporters justify their positions? In your answer, be sure to support your points with historical facts.

Name _____ Class _____ Date _____

Working for Reform

Key Points

- By the early 1800s the Second Great Awakening had sparked a renewed interest in religion in much of the United States.
- Troubled by rapid industrialization, reformers began to direct their efforts toward solving social problems such as alcohol abuse, crime, mental illness, and poverty.
- Support for the abolition of slavery increased during the mid-1800s.
- Through their work in religious and reform movements, women came to see the need to struggle for their own rights and freedoms.

Reviewing Main Ideas

MATCHING In the space provided, write the name of the person identified by each description. Choose your answers from the list below. There is one extra name on the list.

Dorothea Dix   Lyman Beecher   Horace Mann
William Lloyd Garrison David Walker   Susan B. Anthony
Angelina Grimké   Elizabeth Cady Stanton Josiah Quincy

_____ **1.** minister who preached about the evil effects of alcohol

_____ **2.** Massachusetts secretary of education who established a model for free public elementary education

_____ **3.** reformer whose efforts led to the founding of more than 100 hospitals for the treatment of the mentally ill

_____ **4.** prison reformer who fought to establish different places of punishment for children and adults

_____ **5.** free African American businessperson who demanded immediate, universal abolition

_____ **6.** abolitionist whose *Appeal to the Christian Women of the South* urged women to join the abolitionist cause

_____ **7.** women's rights activist who along with Lucretia Mott organized the Seneca Falls Convention

_____ **8.** Quaker reformer who believed that no woman could be free without "a purse of her own"

Name _____ Class _____ Date _____

SHORT ANSWER Provide brief answers for each of the following. Remember to use examples to support your answer.

1. How did the Second Great Awakening affect life in the United States?

_____

_____

2. How did reformers of the early 1800s attempt to help the poor?

_____

_____

3. What tactics did abolitionists use to win support for their cause?

_____

_____

4. Why do you think the Declaration of Sentiments was modeled after the Declaration of Independence?

_____

_____

ORGANIZING INFORMATION

Use the following graphic organizer to explain the connections between the abolition movement and the women's rights movement.

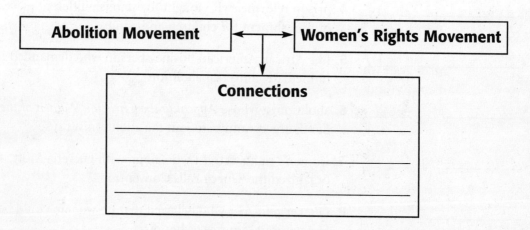

WRITING

Compose a short essay that answers the following question: What was the colonization movement, and why did some white southerners and northerners support it? In your answer, be sure to support your points with historical facts.

Name _____ Class _____ Date _____

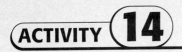 **Reviewing Early American History**

Westward Expansion and Conflict

Key Points

- Texas became an independent republic in 1836 and a state in 1845.
- In the 1840s the United States fought for territory in the Mexican War.
- The promise of trade, a missionary zeal, and the search for religious freedom drew new settlers to the Far West.
- Many more people moved to California after the discovery of gold there in 1848.

Reviewing Main Ideas

TRUE/FALSE Mark each statement *T* if it is true or *F* if it is false.

_____ **1.** The Mexican government encouraged U.S. settlers to come to Texas in order to protect its borders from a U.S. invasion.

_____ **2.** The Texan revolutionaries won victories against the army of General Santa Anna at both the Alamo and Goliad.

_____ **3.** After Texas became a republic, it still faced hostility from Mexico as well as conflicts with local American Indian tribes.

_____ **4.** Opponents of Texas annexation feared that the admission of Texas into the Union would increase the free states' power in Congress.

_____ **5.** The last battle in the Mexican War was fought in Mexico City and was won by the United States.

_____ **6.** With the Gadsden Purchase, the United States acquired parts of present-day Arizona and New Mexico.

_____ **7.** Missionaries who moved to Oregon Country wanted to convert American Indians to Roman Catholicism.

_____ **8.** Mormons in Utah came into conflict with the U.S. government because of the Mormon practice of allowing women to have more than one husband at a time.

_____ **9.** Many of the Spanish soldiers who helped found missions in California married American Indian women and settled permanently in the area.

_____ **10.** Californios scored some of the first major gold strikes in California and forced some miners from the United States off their claims.

Name _____ Class _____ Date _____

SHORT ANSWER Provide brief answers for each of the following. Remember to use examples to support your answer.

1. Why did the Republic of Texas find itself heavily in debt?

_____

_____

2. What were the terms of the Treaty of Guadalupe Hidalgo?

_____

_____

3. What were the terms of the Treaty of Fort Laramie?

_____

_____

4. How did the California Gold Rush affect American Indians living there?

_____

_____

ORGANIZING INFORMATION
Use the following chart to show how major events in the Southwest affected both U.S. settlers and Mexican citizens.

Event	Causes	Effects on U.S. Settlers	Effects on Mexican Citizens
Texas Revolution	1. _____ _____ _____	2. _____ _____ _____	3. _____ _____ _____
Mexican War	4. _____ _____ _____	5. _____ _____ _____	6. _____ _____ _____

WRITING
Compose a short essay that answers the following question: What was manifest destiny, and why did it appeal to many Americans? In your answer, be sure to support your points with historical facts.

Name _____ Class _____ Date _____

Sectional Conflict Increases

Key Points

- The annexation of Texas and U.S. victory in the Mexican War revived the bitter debate over slavery in the western territories.
- Northerners tried to limit the expansion of slavery, while southerners insisted that slavery be allowed to spread into the West.
- The Compromise of 1850 failed to settle the slavery debate, and conflict soon broke out in Kansas.
- Democrat James Buchanan won the presidential election of 1856 after Democrats denounced the newly formed Republican Party as dangerous to the Union.

Reviewing Main Ideas

FILL IN THE BLANK In the space provided, write the name of the person or the historical term that will complete each sentence. Choose your answers from the list below. There is one extra name or term on the list.

Fugitive Slave Act	Pottawatomie Massacre	Henry Clay
John C. Calhoun	Free-Soilers	Wilmot Proviso
Republican	Lecompton Constitution	fire-eaters

1. The southern states threatened to secede if the _____, which would ban slavery in all lands acquired from Mexico, became law.

2. The _____ supported free western homesteads as well as federal funding for internal improvements.

3. Southerners known as _____ held extreme pro-slavery views and supported secession from the Union and a southern confederacy.

4. _____ proposed the Compromise of 1850 to satisfy both northern and southern interests.

5. The _____ made it a federal crime to assist runaway slaves.

6. The _____ ended in five pro-slavery men being brutally murdered by abolitionists.

7. The _____ Party, formed in 1854, was firmly opposed to the expansion of slavery.

8. Kansas's _____ was controversial because it was drafted and passed by pro-slavery delegates only.

Name _____ Class _____ Date _____

SHORT ANSWER Provide brief answers for each of the following. Remember to use examples to support your answer.

1. What is the principle of popular sovereignty, and how did the Kansas-Nebraska Act reflect this principle?

_____

_____

2. Why did both northerners and southerners oppose the Compromise of 1850?

_____

_____

3. Why did the Fugitive Slave Act meet with vigorous opposition in the North?

_____

_____

4. Why did Kansas have two territorial governments competing for control?

_____

_____

ORGANIZING INFORMATION

Use the following graphic organizer to compare how northerners and southerners reacted to the publication of *Uncle Tom's Cabin*.

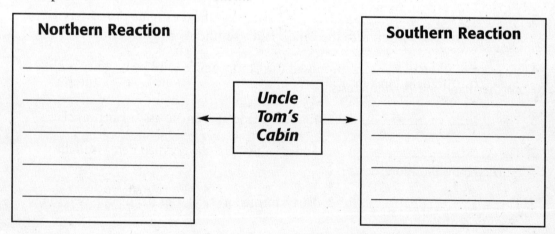

WRITING

Compose a short essay that answers the following question: What were the provisions of the Compromise of 1850? In your answer, be sure to support your points with historical facts.

Name _____ Class _____ Date _____

Reviewing Early American History
On the Brink of War

Key Points

- The 1857 *Dred Scott* decision outraged many people who hoped that the government would be able to prevent the expansion of slavery.
- The conviction and execution of abolitionist John Brown in 1859 fueled sectional tensions.
- After Abraham Lincoln won the presidential election of 1860, South Carolina seceded from the Union.
- Other southern states followed South Carolina's lead, and together the seceded states formed the Confederate States of America.

Reviewing Main Ideas

MULTIPLE CHOICE For each of the following, place the letter of the best choice in the space provided.

_____ 1. This slave sued for his freedom because of his prior residence in a free state and in a free territory.
  a. Roger B. Taney
  b. John Breckinridge
  c. Dred Scott
  d. Robert Purvis

_____ 2. This lawyer ran against Stephen Douglas for a seat in the U.S. Senate.
  a. John Bell
  b. Abraham Lincoln
  c. Jefferson Davis
  d. John Brown

_____ 3. This term refers to Stephen Douglas's belief that the people of a territory have the lawful means to accept or to reject slavery.
  a. People's Law
  b. Freeport Doctrine
  c. Douglas Papers
  d. Articles of Free Will

_____ 4. This abolitionist raided Harpers Ferry.
  a. John Brown
  b. John Breckinridge
  c. John Bell
  d. James Buchanan

_____ 5. Which statement about the 1860 presidential election is correct?
  a. Lincoln carried every state of the Lower South.
  b. Lincoln won the popular vote by a landslide.
  c. Lincoln carried every state of the Upper South.
  d. Lincoln won the electoral vote by a landslide.

_____ 6. This former senator became president of the Confederacy.
  a. Jefferson Davis
  b. James Buchanan
  c. Henry David Thoreau
  d. Roger B. Taney

Name _____ Class _____ Date _____

SHORT ANSWER Provide brief answers for each of the following. Remember to use examples to support your answer.

1. What did Abraham Lincoln mean when he said, "A house divided against itself cannot stand"?

_____

_____

2. How did abolitionists and southern whites react to the raid on Harpers Ferry?

_____

_____

3. Why did the southern states secede from the Union?

_____

_____

4. How did the constitution of the Confederate States of America differ from the U.S. Constitution?

_____

_____

ORGANIZING INFORMATION

Use the following graphic organizer to compare the views of southern secessionists and northerners on the issue of secession.

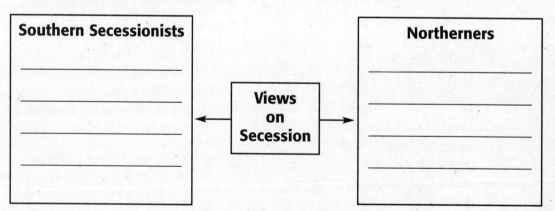

WRITING

Compose a short essay that answers the following question: On what basis did the Supreme Court deny Dred Scott's claim? In your answer, be sure to support your points with historical facts.

Reviewing Early American History

The Civil War

Key Points

- The Confederate attack on Fort Sumter on April 12, 1861, began the Civil War.
- The First Battle of Bull Run in July 1861 made most people realize that winning the war would not be easy.
- In January 1863 the Emancipation Proclamation went into effect, granting freedom to all slaves in Confederate territory.
- In 1863 and 1864 the Union won major victories at Vicksburg, Mississippi; Gettysburg, Pennsylvania; and Atlanta, Georgia.
- Confederate general Robert E. Lee formally surrendered at Appomattox Courthouse on April 9, 1865.

Reviewing Main Ideas

MATCHING In the space provided, write the name of the person or the historical term identified by each description. Choose your answers from the list below. There is one extra name or term on the list.

Ulysses S. Grant	Battle of Gettysburg	Robert E. Lee
Battle of Antietam	Battle of Manassas	David Farragut
William Tecumseh Sherman	Crittenden Compromise	Pickett's Charge

_____ **1.** leader of the Confederate army

_____ **2.** called the First Battle of Bull Run by northerners

_____ **3.** general in chief, commander of all Union forces

_____ **4.** commander of Union warships that seized New Orleans

_____ **5.** bloodiest single-day battle in U.S. military history

_____ **6.** President Lincoln dedicated a national cemetery to the soldiers who fought in this battle

_____ **7.** Confederate attempt to rush the Union center on Cemetery Ridge

_____ **8.** commander who engaged in total war

Activity 17, Reviewing Early American History, continued

SHORT ANSWER Provide brief answers for each of the following. Remember to use examples to support your answer.

1. How did the fall of Fort Sumter affect the relationship between the Union and the Confederacy?

_____

_____

2. How did the military strategies of the North and the South differ?

_____

_____

3. What role did the 54th Massachusetts Infantry play in the war?

_____

_____

4. What were the terms of General Robert E. Lee's surrender?

_____

_____

ORGANIZING INFORMATION
Use the following graphic organizer to describe the results of major battles in the war in the West.

| Fall of Fort Henry and Fort Donelson | → | 1. _____ |

| Battle of Shiloh | → | 1. _____ |

| Surrender at New Orleans | → | 1. _____ |

| Siege of Vicksburg | → | 1. _____ |

WRITING
Compose a short essay that answers the following question: What advantages did each side have at the start of the Civil War? In your answer, be sure to support your points with historical facts.

ACTIVITY 18   Reviewing Early American History

Reconstruction

Key Points

- After the Civil War, the United States struggled to restore the southern states to the Union and to deal with the rights of former slaves.
- The assassination of President Abraham Lincoln on April 14, 1865, left the question of Reconstruction to the new president, Andrew Johnson, and to Congress.
- Although legislation attempted to improve the status of former slaves, African Americans continued to be denied their full citizenship rights.
- At the end of Reconstruction in 1877, the Union was restored.

Reviewing Main Ideas

FILL IN THE BLANK In the space provided, write the name of the person or the historical term that will complete each sentence. Choose your answers from the list below. There is one extra name or term on the list.

segregation	Rutherford B. Hayes	Enforcement Acts
Civil Rights Act of 1875	Civil Rights Act of 1866	amnesty
Plessy v. *Ferguson*	Thaddeus Stevens	Black Codes

1. President Lincoln wanted to offer southerners _____ for all illegal acts that had supported the rebellion.

2. During Reconstruction, southern states passed laws known as _____ to deny African Americans their civil rights.

3. Radical Republican _____ insisted that African Americans be given the right to vote.

4. Even though the _____ declared that everyone born in the United States was a citizen with full civil rights, it did not guarantee voting rights.

5. The _____ enabled the federal government to combat terrorism against African Americans with military force and to prosecute the guilty.

6. The _____ prohibited businesses that served the public from discriminating against African Americans.

7. In the late 1800s southern states passed Jim Crow laws to enforce _____, or separation of the races.

8. In _____ the Supreme Court ruled that segregation was legal as long as the separate facilities were equal.

Activity 18, Reviewing Early American History, continued

SHORT ANSWER Provide brief answers for each of the following. Remember to use examples to support your answer.

1. How did Andrew Johnson's plan for readmitting southern states to the Union differ from that of Abraham Lincoln?

_____

_____

2. What did the Freedmen's Bureau do to help people in the South?

_____

_____

3. What role did the Compromise of 1877 play in ending Reconstruction?

_____

_____

4. How did the sharecropping system hurt southern workers and the southern economy?

_____

_____

ORGANIZING INFORMATION

Complete the following chart by describing the three major Reconstruction amendments to the U.S. Constitution.

Amendment	Purpose
Thirteenth Amendment	
Fourteenth Amendment	
Fifteenth Amendment	

WRITING

Compose a short essay that answers the following question: What were the provisions of the Reconstruction Acts of 1867? In your answer, be sure to support your points with historical facts.